Across the Nullabor

A Journey into the Outback

By Jan Hawkins

ACROSS THE NULLABOR

A Travelogue in the
Around the Campfire Series
By Jan Hawkins

© 2012 Jan Hawkins
All Rights Reserved
ISBN 9780987289698

National Library of Australia Cataloguing-in-Publication entry
Author: Hawkins, Jan.
Title: Across the Nullabor / Jan Hawkins.
ISBN: 9780987289698 (pbk.) **Print Edition**
Series: Around the Campfire ; v. 3 no 2.
Subjects: Australia--Description and travel.
            Nullarbor (S. Aust.)--Description and travel.

Dewey Number: 919.404

    Jan Hawkins reserves the right to be identified as the Author of this work in accordance with the Laws of Copyright. This is an original work of Non-fiction and no part of this publication may be reproduced, stored in a retrieval system or transmitted in any form or by any means, electronic, mechanical, recording or otherwise without the prior written permission of Jan Hawkins.

Join **Jan Hawkins - Writer** on **Facebook**

For other works by Author Jan Hawkins visit

http://janhawkins.com.au

AROUND THE CAMPFIRE

A Travel Log Series on Australia

The **'Around the Campfire'** series is a collection of the tales by writer Jan Hawkins, collected travelling around Australia. The stories are not meant to advertise but are more a collection of anecdotes and recounts of the treasures and tales that can be heard and found on this unique island continent that is Australia.

The spelling of Nullabor has many variations. The Aboriginal Mirning People call this place Oondiri, a place of no water. The English/Latin is Nullarbor means a place of no trees. I would prefer to call it after its long held traditional name of Oondiri, as it indeed has no surface water.

Nullarbor is misleading in that the plain does indeed have trees and brush. It was named by Edmund Delisser in 1865 who was a surveyor for South Australia. Nullabor (as spelt) as used in this book, is the local historical spelling of the plain and I have chosen this interpretation. Perhaps one day we will call the vast expanse of plain after it'd correct traditional name, The Oondiri Plains; and you will know where I mean.

Visit **http://oldiesatlarge.com.au** and discover other adventures to be had around the vast continent

About the Author

JAN HAWKINS

Australian Author, Jan Hawkins, was raised in the Australian bush on the outskirts of Sydney on the Georges River. Now residing in Queensland, she spent 20 years in education at secondary level in the IT field. Her love of computers pales in comparison to her love of the Australian bush and Jan now has quite a portfolio of photographs which are her inspiration. She is passionate about the history of her country and a strong desire to discover and experience new places fuels her desire to travel extensively throughout the land. Along the way she relishes being able to listen to people and to share and enjoy the adventure she calls life.

Jan also writes stories in general and cultural fiction. Her series, 'The Dreaming', is a set of four books which introduce the spiritual culture of the Australian Aborigines. Presented in a contemporary setting The Dreaming stories are a cultural fiction. Readers will delight in being able to follow the lives of the characters such as Ty, the sympathetic shaman of his Community, who falls in love with Aine from the broader multicultural Australian community found in the cities, who becomes his spiritual partner and who in turn becomes immersed in this unique culture.

This stories told in the series explore the characters' lives, their loves and the balance of the world in which we all live. It is a blending of modern culture with the ancient spiritual culture of our indigenous Australians. Introduced in a new contemporary manner are the Spirit Creatures and the Spirit Men and Women who are so much part of The Dreaming.

Jan Hawkins - Writer on Facebook

Visit Author & Writer

http://janhawkins.com.au

HTTP://WWW.WHEREIS.COM/

WHAT POSSESSED ME!

I have always felt that it is not the destination which makes for a memorable holiday, but the journey to get there as well as where ever the destination is. My kids never asked me, *'Are we there yet?'* Or if they did then they got my stock standard answer. *"Yes! We arrived when you planted your toosh on the seat of the car."*

It is the journey, where the trip there is very much part of the holiday and there is no destination more proven to this point than the desire to cross the Nullabor. Regardless of where you intend to end up be it Perth, Kalgoorlie or actually anywhere. This is truly about the journey to get there more than the arrival at any given place.

People in Australia don't say... *'Oh... I'm driving over to Perth.'* What they say is... *'I'm crossing the Nullabor, headed to Perth,'* or where-ever is their destination. This is because the Nullabor is a destination in itself to Aussies; it describes a journey and an adventure. There is only one road which crosses the Nullabor on the southern edge of the continent and it is The Eyre Highway; so named to commemorate the crossing of the Nullabor by Edward John Eyre and his Aboriginal companion and friend, Wylie. They were the only two who survived the difficult crossing in 1840-41.

Touring and travelling independent of motels, without organized commercial guides and with as few demands on my time as possible, or without a strict timetable has always been a passion of mine and this was why I bought a small caravan. I love exploring, discovering the unexpected and quietly feeling the mood of the places I find myself in.

I enjoy the preliminary research of planning a tour, the discoveries of new interests and the adventure of seeking things I like to find; stories untold and experiences yet to be had. But the story of this journey doesn't begin here. In truth it began when my health made me reflect on my goals in life.

When faced with decisions which revolve around your health and your imminent mortality, your focus in life changes. It has always been something of a wonder to me how small decisions in life turn out to be life changing in many respects, particularly when you look back on them.

Such was my decision to adopt my pup who is a small poodle. The choice was easy, poodles have always been a preferred breed of mine in that while they are high maintenance when it comes to grooming, they do not shed their coat, they are generally devoted to their owners and most important they do not require long arduous walks and are

OUR TWO PUPS

animals of comfort primarily, much like myself. So my miniature poodle, Tuppi, entered my life at a time when I needed a daily companion. She was someone who could distract me and keep me company and my thoughts from the challenges I was facing at the time in regards to my health.

Tuppi however was an adventurous hussy, and one dog soon turned into two before we made that ever fateful appointment with the vet. So it was that Scruff Muffin, also known affectionately as Scruffus or Scruff for short, entered our lives. His dad is a wag of a dog that fortunately was a small breed also. A white silky terrier of indiscriminate tastes and habits, who touched our lives briefly and then departed leaving evidence of his visit.

My car, the Maggie, is affectionately known as 'bitsareshitty' in hubby terms or a Mitsubishi as is its more common title, was for a time my primary mode of transport and is even now remembered her with a certain fondness. Hubby is a four wheel drive, utility van enthusiast and somehow a sporty little Magna is just not his cup of tea. However, given a son who bought the car in champagne times and was then reduced to a beer diet, so I inherited the car and the debt in the manner of parents the world over.

It didn't help that me being of a devious bent and son having made the decision to sell his pride and joy, that I decided that I would get him to clean the Maggie first. He did, likely the first time in its entire life and his. He studiously vacuumed and washed the car when I told him that there was a buyer on the horizon waiting to inspect the vehicle. Dutifully at 2pm the buyer arrived on the scene as I had promised... myself and my pen, all ready to have him sign the Maggie over to his mother.

It was then that I discovered that son No.3 had indeed cleaned the car. Unable to remove the dirt as easily as it had accumulated over some two years, son No.3 had used a metal scourer! In the shade he had not noticed the telltale scour marks and it was to be that it was some six months later, after it had been professionally detailed and I was $250 poorer before my Maggie looked as it should have on that fateful and much talked about afternoon. I have learnt that it often never pays to be too smart for your own good.

This is the story of how I became the proud owner of a sporty little Maggie and two entertaining pups. The vintage van followed when I realized that you can't travel far with two pups and no private accommodation. Relatives are fine and some are even tolerant of my 'have car, have dog, will travel' attitude. However one is gifted with only a limited number of like-minded relatives and so it was decided that it was time to look to portable accommodation if I was going to do the visiting and small tours I planned. It had to be the same portable accommodation which I was able to physically manage and something which didn't break the bank.

Hubby is fortunately a tolerant and loving partner in my life's journey and when I announced that I had found just the little van I liked, for a meagre price we could afford, he encouraged me in what others considered was my lunacy. He truly is a special person, and this was even demonstrated more acutely when after purchasing the little van online, I added as an after comment that pick-up would require a weekend trip. He was a little less enamoured when he learnt it would involve a 2000klm (1250 mile) journey across three states which had to be accomplished within three weeks of the purchase date. A lesser man would have crumbled at this point but my faithful life partner *'held it together'* long enough to merely question my sanity in only temperate terms.

Our trip to take ownership of our little van is yet another journey, which for now I will spare you. This was however how I added a cute little twelve foot vintage van to my growing entourage of travel companions; the 'Little Bitch Box' was born. The van was named by the Man, for the pups who demanded to be accommodated en-route. Though many are the people who imagine that the name refers to 'yours truly; blithely not seeing the obvious link with my pups and our history. Then ambiguity is commonly one of my biggest challenges in life, I much prefer the entertainment of the uninformed opinion and in this instance it was a reality which often made me smile.

Our journey across much of the vast expanse that is the Australian continent began because we wished to visit our only bride child who was now expecting an imminent arrival in an addition to their household. The bride child had been enticed from home and hearth by the person she thought was the love of her life, (another story) to live in the remote regions of the Australian desert which gives up the illustrious metal gold to the needs of mankind, and to the industrious miner in the frontier city of Kalgoorlie, Western Australia.

Kalgoorlie is a city situated in the red desert of Western Australia, 5-6 hours drive from the most remote city in the world, Perth. Distance in Australia is commonly measured by 'hours driving' by reason or relativity. It's just simpler that way as travel often needs to be reckoned not only by distance, but by road conditions as well as weather and the type of vehicle you have. Welcome to the world of Australian travel.

This tour involved a life-long desire, the desire of many Aussies and informed tourists to our continent, this is to brave the crossing of the Nullabor Plains and look out over the magnificent cliffs of the Great

THE LITTLE BITCH BOX IN CAMP

Australian Bight. This is an epic car journey of some 4,400klm (2730 miles) one way across the breadth of the continent and we plan to do the round trip.

It is a trip which captures the imagination of a nation's people, even if it is now undertaken on a very organized tar strip within what often ends up being a much disorganized car. It takes on average of three days to cross the Nullabor Plain in tourist time and in any type of comfort. Even getting to what is the "Nullabor Plains" is for many an exercise in braving the remote and adventurous; that is to travel across the Australian continent and across desert lands which are essentially along lonely Outback roads.

Many consider the beginning of the Nullabor crossing to be in the South Australian town of Ceduna. It is indeed the last bastion of civilization and the last reasonable stop for supplies when headed west. It is a stop which is not too much affected too badly by the tyranny of distance. This is until you reach Norseman and Kalgoorlie in WA which is some 1,400klm of desert savannah with little communication, no townships to mention and scattered fuel outposts at measured petrol stops. There is no surface water supply that you can rely on, except when it rains and then no one goes anywhere that is far off that tar strip.

Australia was at this time in the worst drought within reckoning. Our rivers are either born of the vast interior flood-lands and rain catchments or they flow from our mountains. We have the Nations backbone of mountains running down the eastern seaboard. It is from these mountains better known as the 'Great Dividing Range' from which many of our most reliable rivers run. It is our seasonal flood water from the 'wet season' which eventually drain from the north, through the deserts and along ancient water ways which in time spill into the ocean.

This flow of water was something which led our pioneers to believe in the existence of an inland sea. They were wrong and the rivers drained into the great Barcoo system which feeds Lake Eyre, the Darling and River Murray systems and on into the Great Southern Ocean and the Tasman Sea, better known as 'The Ditch' between New Zealand and Australia. These are waterways which can run dry, or flood to make vast oceans of our deserts and outback regions. We aimed to explore and discover some of these inland mysteries along the way, in this time of an all pervading drought.

Preparing our little vintage van for the tour took a few trial runs, tweaking our need for supplies and comfort as well as safety. It was decided that some sort of fly curtain on the van was needed to minimize the invasion of the outback curse. So an old fashioned fly screen door from the 1950-60's era was installed, one which hubby duly built because you simply couldn't buy one the right shape. Our van had also been fitted with a water tank which was generous and the gas lines were checked making sure the small, quaint gas stove of another era in the van was safe.

Being a vintage van, one from circa 1965, screwing and nailing were a part of our ongoing maintenance. The little bond wood van, now clad in aluminium was basically a sound little trailer which offered cosy if not close living. But as small as the little 'Bitch Box' was, we were very happy and very comfortable with our arrangements.

I had learnt the skills in hitching and unhitching the 'Bitch Box' to the Maggie, the demands of the stabilizers and how to tweak the brakes. Backing the Maggie onto the van offered its own challenges but as long as I didn't think about it too much, I managed it. These were also the tasks hubby would mostly undertake, but it is essential that everyone knew how to manage the vehicles. You never know when your skills will be called upon and it is a little late to learn when stranded in the Australian Outback.

My tasks fell to the simpler scope. The management of the pups, food supplies and meals became my focus. Gas for the stove and water supply were also my domain and this involved emergency supplies, a necessity. Safety, first aid and comfort are important considerations and communication, or lack thereof is something also that you need to think about.

The invention of the mobile phone is a boon for Australia and the world but it is a pity that so little of our continent is within range of the communication towers necessary. Vast expanses of our continent are only covered by carrier pigeon or smoke signals and carrier pigeons don't survive well in the desert. So learning how to build a fire is an essential skill which I was taught at an early age along with other basic survival skills. I don't know if I would survive in an emergency situation in the remote areas of our world, but I do know I might be a dam sight more comfortable than I could otherwise have been and this is sufficient for me to travel with some reassurance

We headed out on our adventure with all the excitement that research engenders and the anticipation that accompanies a lifelong ambition in its realization. So it was that we gathered up our good and chattels needed and headed out across the Darling Downs, out on our all Australian adventure.

HEADING WEST ON THE TAR TRACK

Having travelled what is the easy first leg of our trip, we aimed to get at least to the western slopes of the Great Dividing Range and into the area known as the Darling Downs in South East Queensland. The Downs are a beautiful seam of rolling pastures and farming lands. Our first hop was a small one and we left late in the afternoon to begin our trip with this small easy hop.

The Darling Downs was named after a far removed Governor of yesteryear. It is the beginning of the catchment for the Darling River system with the rivers and creeks from here draining down the continent into the Darling River and on into the River Murray.

The Darling Catchment takes in a huge area of southern Queensland and northern New South Wales. Farming here is watered not only by the more erratic flow across the Darling catchment but also by the Great Artesian Basin. This is an ancient artesian remnant of Gondwana Land formed when the water drained down from the Papuan Mountains in an age when the land masses were bridged.

The Darling Downs region is also the land of the 'Goonneeburra Blacks' or 'Fire Blacks', with the European explorers and settlers not arriving until the 1820's; *'goonnee'* being the name for fire and *'burra'* being a generic term for the peoples of the coastal tribes of Moreton Bay area.

These ancient tribes were generally situated around inland Warwick and known for the practice of land management which involved the burning of the grasslands. This was a practice to manage native animal movement and the timely regeneration of the rolling grasslands for which the Darling Downs was renowned. It was an ancient practice which allowed the management of food resources and one which had been going on for so long that even the vegetation had adapted. It was an act however which the settlers frowned upon, often seeing it as a threat to their European farming and husbandry methods. So it was that the wars began.

There is a preconception in Australian history that the Aboriginal tribal people simply allowed European settlers to take land which the indigenous population did not consider their own in any case. This is simply not true, most certainly.

AN ABORIGINAL WARRIOR
(FROM TJAPAKAI FNQ)

Firstly, it is true that the indigenous population did not consider that they owned the land, more that the land owned them. Indeed the Gooneeburra people considered themselves superior in the bush to the Europeans, so much so that they derided their attempts to usurp them on their tribal lands. The warriors demonstrated this by turning their backs in one such incident and slapping their hinds in derision of pursuing party of white men in the 1840's.

In 1843, on the road from Ipswich to the Darling Downs, which is along the route we travelled, the tribal clans once set up a barricade of logs. When the drays were stalled the warriors then attacked. They had hidden in the nearby brush with the aim which had been expressed on more than one occasion; that to starve out the settlers on the Darling Downs by effectively blocking their supplies.

The Aborigines in the district created much havoc by raiding acres of grain, harvesting it for their own needs in much the same way as they had for millennia. In one incident drowning whole herds of cattle in retribution of their eating out grasses grazed on by the native animals and thus denuding the district of native game. In this way they undoubtedly felt they were managing the land in a time when it was overstocked with animals, needless to say the settlers found this event upsetting.

Compliant adversaries the natives were not… anymore than the colonists and emigrants were. It was a time of cultural ignorance on both parts which led often to bloodied clashes between people trying to survive or build a new life under a new circumstance.

One of the greatest early mysteries for our growing colony, some 150-200 years ago was that of the 'Inland Sea'. This was believed to be a vast ocean which as it was imagined, was to the west of the Great Dividing Range the might of which runs the entire east coast of Australia.

Why they imagined there was such an ocean or sea was because, as mentioned the rivers ran west on the other side of the mountain range and their reasoning was that this would naturally lead to a ocean off to the west. The rivers though drain the entire length of the continent, some 3,000klm and this was something which they didn't expect at all. The only oceans they found were those of bull dust and creeping sandhills and the savannah of the central deserts.

Imagine always coming to these sands and expecting they would lead eventually to the ocean shoreline; it was just a matter of traversing them to where they would find the inevitable ocean waters. And so it was that so many of our early explorers died. Such was the folly of men who came from another world, another land, while this land defied the logic which was born in a northern experience.

AN EXAMPLE OF SETTLERS HOMES IN THE OUTBACK

A NOTE ON OUR EXPLORERS

Australia seems to have attracted more than its fair share of intrepid if not inept European explorers in its colonial years. Many ended up as parched bones in our Outback, or were the cause of the number of parched bones of others which could be found in the Outback.

I have never understood how it could be that such characters, who were often men who had fled the label of mediocrity in their homelands could lay claim to the deeds which they do. They arrived here in the hope of finding fame if not fortune in the newly settling colony and for some reason we have accorded them fame which is questionable. This is despite their many failures and despite our neglect to recognize the knowledge and guidance of the Aboriginal people who blazed the way before them. Perhaps they were chasing the glory of the great navigators and explorers of the age before their own.

I have always felt that it was the homesteaders, and those who truly battled and fought to survive the many hardships that should be afforded the title of Explorers. These were the people and families who often opened up the vast inlands even before the Government of the day recognized their value, if not the extent of their existence. People like the young Jardine sons of Far North Queensland, the Kidman family and so many more who are truly not recognized or even much noted.

Ludwig Leichhardt was one of the many curious European blokes who made a claim to glory and was accorded this accolade. He travelled this region we were now passing through; his three main expeditions leaving from the Darling Downs which was the last outpost at the time, this being Jimbour Station near the Bunya Mountains.

On Leichhardt's fateful third expedition, he hoped to travel across the continent to where Perth is today or there abouts on the western seaboard, revisiting his failed 1st attempt at this, which was only his 2nd expedition. He was an eccentric Prussian (German), a naturalist who although working hard in his studies also never managed to earn his own living. He regarded himself as something of a gentleman and explorer and he paid the price for what some would consider his folly. To this day what became of him and his last entourage remains a mystery.

Ludwig explored vast regions of the eastern coast on his own after his arrival into what he considered undoubtedly the squalor of young Sydney Town. He longed for a companion of like interests as seen by his letters to friends, but the mystery of the Australian bush and exploration had enraptured him as it did others even in these days. Although it was reckoned by many that he was not a bushman of any skill and many of his companions met with an ill fate because of this.

Going home to Prussia for Ludwig was not an option as he was avoiding the obligatory military service and would have been gaoled for his neglect having officially become a military deserter in 1840. Instead he found friends and admirers in the Australian wilderness, one far removed from Europe and he spent much of his time living on the generosity of others. He cut an increasingly eccentric figure as he explored the forests of the eastern coastal ribbon indulging his botanical interests. He had made his way to the settlement of Brisbane by early 1843, mooching on missionaries, Aboriginals and settlers alike. Having spent two years in Australia he had not managed to earn a single penny.

In 1848 Ludwig set out for the third and last time on his expedition to a destination that was eventually to become Perth. A fanciful expedition of the era as expressed by local stockmen and others invited to become involved. Indeed one of his mentors, A W Scott, a wealthy 'squatter' from the Newcastle region in NSW tried to teach Ludwig some bush-craft, but instead described him as 'having little sense of direction, no self-reliance and no resource'. He was a man reputed to have been 'able to get lost in George Street, Sydney Town'. Never the less he went onto a questionable historical fame as an Australian explorer entering folklore after completing an over-long and difficult expedition across the north of the continent from what is now the trek from Brisbane to Darwin.

Much of Australian history is questionable I have found, having been written by those with an eye to fame and notoriety or hope of credibility.

The proposal for Leichhardt was to travel from east to west across the continent, the same as we now proposed some 150 years later. Leichhardt was massively equipped with several men, including a few Aboriginal men. One being Wommai (believed to also be known as Harry Brown) who was a native from the Newcastle tribal group in NSW and who had been Ludwig's companion on past expeditions. They had some 20 mules and 270 goats for milk and meat, six horses and fifty bullocks. He carried enough food, medicine and ammunition for two years. He however, managed to vanish from the face of the land along with his entourage and to this day his remains or evidence of his expedition has never been found. I trust we will meet with more success on our own journey.

In 1860, another ill fated and ill considered expedition led by Bourke and Wills who attempted to cross the continent from south to north. Although not directly associated with a search for Ludwig, they did however manage to stimulated interest in Leichhardt's destiny. While others searched for what became of them. The Bourke and Wills expedition was also one of monumental disaster of epic proportions.

However there is the tale of the 'wild white man' living with the natives on the Barcoo in the far west desert region of Queensland which captures the imagination. Reputed to be a member of the ill-fated Leichhardt expedition it is thought he had managed to survive some 22 years after the disappearance of Leichhardt. The Queensland government engaged a Mr J L Gilmour who was a sub-inspector of the Native Mounted Police at Bulloo Barracks of the far west region of Queensland, and who was an exceptional bushman, to check out the tale. At Wantata waterhole they found evidence of white men meeting an ill-fate when they discovered unburied skeletons and other scraps. However nothing conclusive was ever found to discover just who the 'wild white man' was or even to verify his existence; nor even to indicate whom the skeletons may have been.

THE GREAT WESTERN PLAINS OF QUEENSLAND

The greater western plains are vast, and it is easy to see the lay of the land about you. It is a world where there are no fences along the paddocks or little to distract the eye for great distances. It seems mostly to be or vast fields of what is prime farming land. Tomorrow we will venture fully into west of the *Great Divide* and across into Northern NSW, but for the moment we are settled in a lovely camp just out from Millmerran, west of Toowoomba called the Yarramalong Weir.

Millmerran is the end of the line so to speak, at least this rail line, as it travels no further while the roads take us south into the northern plains of New South Wales.

There is a rail line that carries on through to Dalby further west, and several rail lines branch out from Dalby travelling as far west as Charleville, but for the main south eastern line, it is the end of the line.

New South Wales and Queensland are pretty crap at sharing as with much of our bureaucracy and when all is said and done they have a different gauge of rail line which essentially means a NSW train will not run into Queensland and vice-versa. Makes you wonder if the states ever really agreed on anything.

As we cross the western State border between NSW and Queensland we will move into the savannah and malley country of North Western NSW. I am looking forward to crossing the Darling River in a day or two, before we reach Broken Hill at the extreme west and outback of NSW and the city known as 'Silver Town' in its early history, as we venture west down and across the continent towards Western Australia.

For tonight the night is still but for the noisy bugga down near the weir who is running a generator and insists on driving the short walk to the loo every 25 minutes! I have a hearty dislike of generators, terribly intrusive machinery which should be banned from quiet places at unreasonable hours. If you can't live without a generator running most of the time then you should confine yourself to the city centres or caravan parks. Or at the very least run them only to charge battery banks and not chunder them into the quiet of the night disturbing not only fellow campers but wildlife, not to mention the pollution they cause.

But it is a glorious night despite our inconsiderate neighbour and a great spot to begin our transcontinental adventure camped on the banks of the Condamine River, west of the Great Divide.

The little 'Bitch Box' is travelling well and being so small it is hardly noticeable behind the Maggie. Tuppi my pup, on the other hand doesn't much like the caravan that follows so close and spends much of her time keeping a wary eye on the intrusive follower, while Scruff simply vies for attention when attention is on the offering.

WALLABY OF THE WESTERN PLAINS

FISH FOR DINNER ON THE RIVERS WEST OF THE DARLING DOWNS

The pups snuggle at night with us in the little van and warn us of any intrusions outside, strange noises and the late arrival of other travellers in camp. Travelling with pups has definite advantages even if it means that many of our National Parks are excluded from our itinerary. Weighing up the advantages and disadvantages of their company is an annoyance, however fortunately this time our pups are a welcome company as I really hate when I have to leave them behind.

THE STATE BORDER: INTO NEW SOUTH WALES

Crossing the Macintyre River today was a highlight of our day after a slow beginning with the dawn. The Macintyre feeds into the Darling Murray catchment and also acts as the border between Queensland and New South Wales so we are now in the New South Wales State and travelling through the mid western regions.

We crossed the border at Goondiwindi and spent a little time exploring the town which has a country charm. Most interesting was the levee banks which the town had built against the floods which the river brings and in the small museum there we found many photo's of past floods which the town had experienced. This was in the old customs house which was also known as the 'Border House' built in 1850 before the separation of Queensland and New South Wales.

Goondiwindi is one of fourteen border posts and was originally the teamster's camp, established before Federation in 1901 to maintain tariff dues on traffic and trade between the States. Customs duty was an important form of revenue for the struggling colonies and not something that local authorities could live without. Particularly with all the pastoral developments occurring in south western Queensland and western regions of New South Wales at the turn of the century.

I never realized we had smugglers in our history but indeed there are. Smuggling goods across the borders a century and a half ago was a lucrative trade. Queensland was proclaimed a colony in 1859, free of New South Wales and sorely in need of revenue due to a bit of early 'big city' pilfering in Brisbane.

The governing body decided that they were missing out on some revenue with the flow of goods, namely tea and tobacco between the colonies. Duties were considerably higher in Queensland than in New South Wales; and it was Queensland that would profit the greatest due to the greater flow of goods from New South Wales than that which went the other way. As such the border custom's crossing was born after the introduction of the Customs Act in NSW.

Goondiwindi was the border joint of 3 large holdings which produced mainly wool. The bullocky teams would travel overland from Maitland on the coast near Newcastle, a trip of some 600klm (380 miles) which is a long way with a bullocky team travelling the speed of a cow. This all to trade their much needed goods for wool and then make the return run back to trade again another day.

Where the three stations met, is where the bullocky teams would hole up waiting for their return goods and as such it developed into a township.

They are also very proud of the race horse the Goondiwindi Grey which most city people will remember. Gunsynd being the winner of a Melbourne Cup 1972 and the best grey racer in Australian history with a will to win that was magnificent to behold, one of our lovely racers after the heart of Phar Lap.

Leaving the town we moved onto follow the path of the Gwydir River and into the town of Moree which sits on the Gwydir. It is most renowned for their thermal hot springs drawn from the great artesian basin or aquifer which sits under most of Queensland and half of New South Wales.

It seems that many of the major towns are fed by the major rivers which flow down from the Great Dividing Range westward, eventually draining into the Darling Murray River system. Water is indeed the source from which our civilization prospers and it is for this reason that the drought strikes so hard in the heart of the land.

The next major town on is Narrabri which sits on the Namoi, and these are the major towns of the catchment plains. The inland sea of rolling grasslands which is flat, flat and flatter is very subject to flooding. They seem to produce cotton and wheat mostly around the district on what are these flood plains, a testament to the endless ribbon of paddocks.

PEAKS OF THE WARRUMBUNGLE'S

The only exception to the level expanse of land is the mountains cast to the East of us which have been in view for most of the day. These mountains are the Mastermans Range visible around Narrabri. Towards the end of the day we had moved into the foothills of the beautiful Warrumbungle's which are mountains into which the township of Coonabarabran nudges.

The Warrumbungle's are a magnificent range of striking beauty and we are nestled into the foot of these ranges. They are the ancient remnant of a huge shield volcano which has narrow sloping sides like a ancient warriors shield of Nordic origins and are a famous part of this wonderful landscape. It was 15 million years ago when these volcanoes were last active and it was this that created their distinctive presence on the flood plain.

Crossing the Warrumbungle Range and dropping down onto the lowland plains of the Barrier Highway, we head into Cobar in central west of NSW. We are deep in the New South Wales Outback which is so much part our land; yet which so few visitors to our country see these places in their pursuit for sun, sand and surf. It is beautiful country out here, wild, free and breathtaking in its isolation.

This region is of volcanic origins and is extremely old. It is part of the catchment for the northern river systems, The Paroo to the west is the most pristine of river ways and one still in its natural state as a wild river, it is also considered the major river system for the Darling. We can only hope that it will always remain that way, as it is one of the healthiest wild river systems on our continent.

HEADED WEST OF COBAR NSW

Driving up into the hills of the Warrumbungle's was markedly different to coming up off the level landscape of the western plain. The scenery changed to one of forest, where stands of the native Cyprus pines nestled all around you. To be found here is evidence of the ancient volcano cores which fed the western plains with their rich soil as they eroded down over the millennia leaving only their hard lava cores and the undulating hills which make up the mountain range. These magnificent ranges are peppered with clusters of rocks and tor's from the volcanoes which were active 15-18 million years ago.

The small grey kangaroos in the area have a reputation for being very tame, although wild running and they are a delight to the visitors and it is a great place to make a stop or take a break. Climbing down from the range you could see why the mountains are noted as being quite beautiful and the savannah and malley lands which comprise the western plains grow to once more become flat and flatter.

As we travel we tend to camp out at the many free camps and roadside stops along the way like so many others. This is mainly because they are convenient, generally safe and offer the opportunity to enjoy the bush without the bustle of a town.

The Newell Highway along which we have been travelling for most of the day is also known as the road train route for good reason. It was a busy night last night and I learnt that you can actually sleep next to a train line, particularly when it is a highway and they are road trains.

A few times during the night I found myself sitting up and groping for the curtains as I swear we were going to get run over… but no; we were fine and next time we will find a spot more off the road train route where all the b-doubles run.

These trucks are huge and they tow two or more trailers behind as they move goods along the inland routes in a day or a night's work. They also make for light sleep. Hearing these monster road trains bearing down on you and then hopefully continuing into the night can be just a tad disturbing. But watching them manoeuvre these monsters around the little van as they pull in for a break is heart stopping. It takes stronger nerves than I have!

Arriving into the township of Nyngan is when you realized you are once more back on the north western Outback plains well and truly. Most of the townships to the west of the Warrumbungle's have built flood levees around the towns in an attempt to preserve them from the floods which drain down in the wet season from northern Queensland, travelling thousands of miles. However Nyngan, which is noted as a flood town, has a helicopter flood evacuation reserve just outside the town which really bought the message home to us. It all seemed as flat as a tack... but evidently there were levels of flat where the flood waters are concerned.

The whole township was evacuated in 1990 floods when torrential rains in Queensland moved south, running west of the Great Divide. The populace was ferried by helicopter holus-bolus to Dubbo, 160klm away when the hastily complemented levees were breached and much of the town was inundated.

Getting into Coonabarabran, also known as the Astronomy Capital of Australia because of its observation telescopes and remarkably clear night sky's, offers a fascinating history. We spent part of the morning discovering the Diprotodon which is a dinosaur, of the mega-fauna age who had been dug up locally. A charming big blighter he was too... they found him, or rather dug him up in 1979 and most notable is his skull which is about half the size of me, so he was no small chappie. Although the rest of him was also scattered here about and is now on display in the Information centre.

This guy is known as the Tambar Springs Diprotodon and is on permanent loan to the city of Coonabarabran which I think is commendable rather than being stuffed in some remote museum for the coastal folk. He just simply belongs here. He was the largest marsupial to have ever lived and his closest relatives are believed to be wombats and koala's

Australia is Earths oldest continent continuously above water and Diprotodon fossils are found in many places across Australia. They were the largest of the mammals in this land.

Named for its two forward teeth and resembling a rhino without a horn, they stood several feet tall and were some 1-2½ ton which is a lot of weight to throw

around. He had fur like a horse, unlike being as bare skinned as a rhino and was somewhat pigeon toed like a wombat. They had a backward facing pouch for their young like a wombat and dined on mostly grasses, trees and shrubs.

The oldest known fossils are some 1.6 million years old. They ranged across forests, open woodlands and scrub and are believed to have begun to die out some 25,000 years ago, give or take 2,000 years. They coexisted on the continent along with man and it is thought that they were still hunted on the Liverpool plains of N.S.W. 7,000 years ago.

I guess he was like a big cuddly wombat with long legs though you would have had a hard time cuddling him as he was the girth of a rhino and the size of a horse.

The western plains of NSW are, once you get into them, true malley country and the soil is markedly red. As you approach Cobar which is smack in the middle of what is known as the Barrier Highway (named for the Barrier Mountain Range in which Broken Hill sits) you feel truly isolated.

Cobar is a mining town, mining gold and copper and still is productive in copper today. It also has flood levees and their

THE MODERN DAY WOMBAT

world is dirt red. Most notable aside from the mine heads and the old township centre itself, are the small herds of wild goats which roam through the malley and it was out from Cobar that we clocked up our 1,000klms so far on this trip.

At the moment we are parked halfway between Cobar and Wilcannia on the Barrier Highway and by tomorrow we hope to be in Broken Hill. Broken Hill is in the fruit fly exclusion zone so we aren't permitted to carry any fruit or soft type veggies into the zone and there are signs evident to this effect. I don't know I they still have the fly gates but we will find out tomorrow and as we have been caught before and lost our tomatoes. Then this time I have made sure we had eaten any likely candidate for confiscation before we got here.

It is quite a pleasant spot where we are camped near the dry river bed of red sand and we have about half a dozen vans about the rest area so far which are other travellers who have pulled in for the night. One of our favourite travellers is Matilda on the jumbuck, who we saw today... they called her 'Dunafarmin' which is cryptic Aussie lingo that doesn't take much to figure out.

OUR RIVER CAMP SITE

OUTBACK NSW

The Outback... even the name conjures up a romantic view, or so I had thought. Wilcannia is enough to disabuse you of this unfortunately. Where do you begin to describe Wilcannia of today? It didn't frighten me at all but then I have matured enough over the years not be threatened easily... it is after all just a very small settlement of several hundred people on the edge of the Darling River which of course drains into the River Murray and as far up the river as many of the old paddle steamers will or would have travelled in wetter seasons. Over 50% of the population are indigenous and it seems a large proportion of the people spend their day either waiting for the pub to open, or waiting for someone to return from the hotel. If ever there is a place that needed a community heart, it is Wilcannia as we find it today.

Here at Wilcannia the paddle steamers of old would pick up their burden of wool and take it down stream on its way to Adelaide or Melbourne. Of course now-a-days the paddle steamers no longer ply the Murray and the Darling with goods and indeed the Darling is as dry as a bone at the moment with the drought, but Wilcannia has lived on in better days and now it is crumbling in ruin.

It is the type of place you prefer not to even stop due to the over burden of the people with little to do. This describes the apparent temper of the small town with its dilapidated and unloved state more than enough to warn you, then the burnt out buildings and the crumbling stone work of old does speak of a community unloved. Graffiti walls warn you, if the small group of people seemingly permanently at ease in the park and outside the pub doesn't. The only commercial interest in the town seems to centre on the one open and boarded hotel and a struggling petrol stop nearby. You can see how it has fallen to disrepair, and it is one of the better buildings.

Wilcannia…? not a place I would chose to stay… or even stop. I looked at Wilcannia and thought of Echuca which is the other end of the paddle steamer line. Echuca is a glorious town on the River Murray. It transports you back to yesteryear and is a town to commend. It is evidence of what can be done to illustrate a romantic and engrossing history of colonial times. We visited Echuca last year on our run to pick up the little Bitch Box from South Australia; and we fell in love with the town. Wilcannia is the exact opposite, it is the end of the same line and it is everything that it should never have developed to be.

BUILDINGS IN WILCANNIA MAIN STREET

When we pulled into the petrol stop we immediately attracted the attention of a belligerent man across the street who made haste towards the garage driveway for no apparent reason but in a indecent effort to park his wheel chair in the path of our car, not two metres from the front bumper. He was joined by another woman with a pram who made a b-line for the back of the van and happily held a loud conversation in dialect shouted between the two, the pram positioned to block our exit. I am not a person give to fanciful imaginings, I know when I am targeted and a target we had unwittingly become.

I watched in fascination, their obvious interest at what they considered was our apparent dilemma and wondered how often this same situation had been visited and how one could extract yourself from such a situation without giving offence or being overbearing as the townspeople mentioned were attempting to be. I considered our options and quietly settled for a sit-out wondering what hubby would make of the situation when he emerged from the garage shop into where he had vanished a few minutes ago. The minutes ticked on.

Neither the man, nor his accomplice had seen hubby fill the tank and head off to pay for the petrol, approaching as they had from an angle and with a haste that blocked their view, and at the time I gave it all little account as the minutes ticked on.

Hubby emerged, now he is a patient and kindly soul and he too would have waited till dark for the problem to resolve itself rather than offend another soul. But it was the look on the man's face as he seen my man emerge that left me wondering how it would have all ended if my man had not been himself of a apparent Aboriginal appearance.

The look of surprise was what struck me most, and then with a short word in dialect to the woman behind the van, the man moved off on his way as Hubby climbed into the car with a nod and a frown of confusion having just realized that the pair were positioned oddly and for no apparent reason... all rather intriguing.

If necessary I was prepared to sit there all day and wait; we were in no hurry and the attention of the groups of men in the park opposite was enough to warn me that this was not a new dilemma for a passing traveller. But I was left wondering what was the anticipated outcome of the whole and it is experiences like this that leave me with a question in my mind and a distaste in my mouth. I guess it was some type of small town entertainment for those that seem to have little else to do.

We had topped up our petrol at a price which was inflated to around 25 cents more per litre than anywhere else, but here your choices are few and far between. So you top up where you can when you have the added burden of a van... so we did want to ensure we had enough fuel aboard. We drove around and then headed out of the town... glad to have left the experience behind and wondering at what would have been played out in other circumstances.

THE DARLING RIVER AS WE FOUND IT

Here is the mighty Darling River it is as dry as a bone at the moment, even though there has been local rain it hasn't made it to here. One day I hope to see the Darling in flow again, as it flowed a century ago but it will take wiser politicians and bureaucrats than we have had to date and we will just have to wait on the flooding rains. The centre span of the bridge actually opens up to allow the paddle steamers through; bet that hasn't worked for a while.

The tribal people of the Darling here were known as the 'River People' or the Barkindji or the vanished tribes of the lower Darling River Region. A tribe wise to the ways of the weather and land, respected people amongst the other tribes, a people with tribal customs and specialized skills. The held an ancient knowledge which allowed them to survive in the often inhospitable desert regions, renown as they were for their superior weaponry. They lived and traded into the western desert and ranging as far north as present day Queensland following the ancient rivers in trade and custom.

THE EMU OF THE WESTERN PLAINS

Some of the Barkindji people in time moved to work on the large stations of the settlers, others were to be found in missions outside their tribal lands and many lost their way from tribal living as their lives changed, some becoming part of the problem bought on by colonization even in the remote regions and adding largely to the itinerant population of the early colony along with the convicts who failed to settle.

Disease and warfare took a terrible toll decimating the Aboriginal tribes after they had survived for some 45,000 years previous. This tribal group drew its name from the Barka, which was the name for the river for time immemorial before someone decided it was to be called the Darling River 170 years ago. The Barkindji began to lose their grip on their traditional lands as early as the 1830's as settlers moved up along the River Murray and the Darling River. The European settlers were also facing extinction in the region due to bad farming practices imported from Europe and many faced starvation both native and colonist.

Many of the Aboriginal tribe suffered along with the least educated and often the most socially disadvantaged peoples of the townships. By 1936 many of the Barkindkji living on missions were bought back onto, or nearby their tribal lands to help preserve their cultural heritage but it was something of a band-aid solution. Those who fared best were those who were not brought in from missions and reserves, but those who could earn a wage and living along with the settlers and then still practice their tribal customs within their land. These people managed to retain some of their cultural heritage.

The run from Wilcannia to Broken Hill was interminable and seemed to go on forever as the distance shimmered in the heat. The red earth flood plains, which were peppered with salt bush spread out before you, everywhere you looked; relieved only by the occasional tree. The malley scrub of yesterday fell away to the savannah grass lands and salt bush, and on what is the Darling flood plain we found the small groups of emu, flocks of galah and the occasional whopper of an eagle feasting on road kill. Goats galore were still around and sheep put in an occasioned appearance in small flocks.

Kangaroo's were mostly road kill unfortunately, as they feed at dusk and dawn on the grasses as the side of the road. They are mostly nocturnal creatures so they tend to meet the road trains. We learnt that a *'Wilcannia shower'* is actually a dust storm and we have driven through one or two of those also.

We approached Broken Hill after what seemed like hours and laughed at the thought that the Barrier Range, in which Broken Hill is nestled, had actually named that because an explorer felt it was a barrier to his progress north. As the range runs north to south, I suspect that the guy was lost.

The range seems to me to be a collection of rolling hills and we have decided to take a lay day and explore Broken Hill and its surrounds as it seems that there is just so much to see in the area. So we chose one of the caravan parks and have settled ourselves for two nights. The dogs of course are pleased for a break in the travelling and so are we. So tomorrow we will explore Broken Hill or "Silver City" and a little ghost town some 25klm out of town called Silverton.

THE FLOOD PLAINS OF THE DARLING

BROKEN HILL – OUTBACK NSW

Broken Hill is a silver mine. The mine head is smack in the middle of the town which in Australia doesn't seem at all odd. It doesn't add much to the scenery though, but it certainly defines the town. The houses notably are largely made of corrugated iron in that there is no lumber about so wood is not easy to come by and the streets are wide in the manner of old townships more accustomed to those bullocky teams, but it is a prosperous town and we are looking forward to exploring it.

A bit of local history I found funny was the tale of how the town came by its water. When silver (and a few other metals) were discovered around 1885 the town virtually grew up overnight. Water became a major consideration... particularly as there wasn't any. So they called in the Afghan

CAMELS OF THE DESERT

cameleers and they bought water up from the lakes nearby with camels, namely Lake Menindee, some considerable distance south east.

The Afghan's tended to settle outside the town in that there were large numbers of these desert traders as there was a great need to supply the town with water. They tended to create small settlements on the edge of town which were called Guan-towns.

This collection of tin humpies and all manner of make do materials were actually called *'tinnies'* and they went on to become the main building materials for the town.

However the story has a sad ending to it. With World War 1 we of course were fighting the Turks and amongst the Afghan cameleers were a smattering of Turks.

In 1915 it was this situation which led to the only enemy attack Australia suffered on Australian soil… (the air raids on Darwin and Broome and elsewhere were from the air and those In Sydney and elsewhere were by

AN EXAMPLE OF THE AFGHAN TINNIE

sea). However in Broken Hill there were two local Afghan's, one with strong Turkish links and they took exception to the Aussies and decided to attack the local rail line. They fired on a train from a ice-cream cart and the assault caused pandemonium as well as injuries, some serious. The two Afghan snipers were unfortunately killed in a rout by the local constabulary which is a sad conclusion, as tragic in some ways as those injured in the attack.

The local water pipeline from Lake Menindee was built finally in 1952, some 109klm of it, which sounded the death knoll for the Afghan cameleers and all that remains now in Broken Hill of their memory are the *'tinnies'* of the town which are scattered everywhere.

We are just a hop-skip-an-jump from the South Australian border and soon we will cross over into South Australia. We have already crossed the first time zone and gained a half an hour. Not that we are setting our watches back yet, the challenge is to remember just how much we are out of sync with home.

Broken Hill has been filled with a lot of enjoyment. I continually find touring the streets enchanting with their curious 'tinnies' and odd architecture to amuse us.

The mine head is smack in the middle of the town and makes for some interesting photo's with the large mountains of overburden growing towards the sky in Broken Hill central. Hubby has ventured down into the bowels of the earth with a tour of the Delprats Mine, which was originally the BHP mine first developed around the mid 1880's and we all know about BHP. He loved it and the dill forgot to take the camera so following are his recounts.

He dropped 4 levels, 420 metres via a cage and there he was introduced to the pneumatic drill which they actually started up. It was explained how they work in a 2 man team below the earth, and in a 6 man gang which is individually contracted to the mine by private negotiation; and what they dig is negotiated via personal contract.

They dig the silver laden stone with little hydraulic bobcats and the 'team' is everything. They are actually paid by the ton they dig out... anything from 15-20 cents a ton which seems an incredibly small amount but they do manage to make very impressive pay. So they must dig heaps! Rotating in 3 shifts over 24 hours the team of six works an 8 hour spell.

The Delprats mine is actually due to close next month as they are going to be digging deeper and under what is now the rail yards, so they will use the old mine as ventilation tunnels and as such they will be closed and tours will no longer be running.

Venturing out to Silverton, which is described as a *'ghost town'* 25klm out of Broken Hill was well worth it. To me a 'ghost town' is a fully deserted town where I would expect to meander around at my heart's content amongst dilapidated buildings; Silverton is not this. Such is its attraction as a *'ghost town'* that people are now setting up commercial interests for tourist trade which comes along on the tour busses. The local pub was in full swing, and there are a number of other commercial ventures such as galleries, opal shops and commercial tours through the gaol.

SCENE FROM SILVERTON GHOST TOWN

MAD MAX REPLICA AT SILVERTON

The town was featured in the Mad Max film and we came across Mad Max's souped up car parked outside the hotel. One of the real curiosities of the old town is the *'coroner's bath'* in the gaol though, which is now a museum. This was filled with preservative and the bodies were placed into it until the coroner came from Sydney. This in the days before the railway and it could take up to 3 months for the coroner to arrive.

A reminder of the days of the cameleer are the camels on the outskirts of town, they are now for the tourists to ride although there are wild camels about but we have not seen them to date.

The camels looked well cared for and Silverton was a place of many cameleers so it is aptly located. Most of the homes here have been driven into disrepair but what I found most amusing was the for sale signs giving rise to optimism. Many of the old stone houses will end up another commercial venture for sure, but it was such an amusing combination in the middle of no-where that I couldn't resist commenting on it.

We have enjoyed our little sojourn in Broken Hill and tomorrow we head off into South Australia, crossing the border and head off into the Flinders Ranges. The Flinders Ranges are a favourite of ours and this will be our fourth venture into them. They are simply stunning with lots of little stop spots and meandering creeks and historic towns.

As you pass through the scenery of the plains with the Flinders Ranges on the approach, it is here you appreciate how a painter can do better justice to a scene than a photographer.

The Ranges have a distant flush of green which contrasts with the red earth plains forming what seems to be almost in a silhouette in some lights, streaked as they are with the yellowed grass at the foot of the range.

The only shame is that we won't be spending more time in these ranges as we are considering a diversion into the Eyre Peninsula south west of Port Augusta. This is fully dependant on the weather as there is a cyclonic low moving across the Great Australian Bight which could mean bad weather... as in seriously bad; so we will save judgment for tomorrow and see how the weather swings.

As we progress into the more remote regions in the next few days we will arrive at the edge of the Nullabor. One thing is that we are definitely gaining an appreciation of what is meant by the expression that this is a *'bloody big country'*... there is so much I would return to explore; and so much of so very little to amuse when given such a huge distance to travel. It is a very odd combination filled with oddities that make this part of the world so unique and so enjoyable.

VIEW OF THE FINDERS RANGE SA

THE WEDGED TAIL EAGLE

Heading out from Broken Hill, back down into the red earth savannah and saltbush was like stepping back into yesteryear with Mad Max. As the hours rolled away with the miles we kept an eye out for wildlife, catching glimpses of kangaroos, emu's and the amazing savannah eagles. These eagles are striking, standing the height of a 2yr old and up to the height of a 4yr old child, they are not to be messed with. They feed on road kill and as the day was not an overly hot one, they were out in force.

SUNSET IN THE FLINDERS RANGE SA

We saw several large eagles and we had the need to be conscious of them when we stopped for a cuppa or a break as the dogs would be considered small enough for a good feed and these guys were on the prowl. They nest in this season and would likely be feeding young. They are absolutely magnificent and you can't do justice to their magnificence with a camera on the red earth plain. So I have included a photo of an eagle taken in a tamer environment

The Flinders Ranges are a lovely experience after the red salt bush of the plains. The soft green hills rolled on. Peterborough which you pass through is *'railway central'* and one of the few places where the three different gauges of rail line used by the different States meet. The wider gauge is from the north meeting the eastern gauge and the smaller western gauge rail; all coming to a turntable which catered for the lot to them in Peterborough. It was a quaint and interesting little town.

The pass in the south Flinders Ranges was remarkable and provides a rare view of Spencers Gulf as you start your descent down the other side of the range. The blue waters are spread out before you like the corner of a picnic blanket. The Gulf is some 322klm (200 miles) long and over 100klm wide at its mouth and is named by Flinders in 1801 after some English Earl related to Princess Diana. Settlement around the Gulf didn't happen until the late 1840's after Edward John Eyre's exploration of the region. Other people also named the Gulf, but it was Capt. Flinders naming which gained popularity.

SUNSET OVER SPENCERS GULF

CLEVE- THE EYRE PENINSULA S.A.

There are pockets of light rain, a consequence of the low moving across to the south of the State and this bought an amazing flush of subtle purple where the rain was gathering and falling over the ranges and onto the flood plains. It was simply beautiful.

With the low moving across the Southern Ocean bringing an incredible squall around Victor Harbour in the far south east of South Australia and rain with high winds into the western and southern ranges we decided to push on to the Eyre Peninsula to the south west of Port Augusta.

This is an area we have never ventured and are looking forward to exploring. On route we were told of an exceptional freebie camp in the centre of the Eyre Peninsula in the small mountain cluster to be found just west of Cowell which is on the east coast of the peninsula.

The *'Grey Nomads'* freely trade info. on good stops and in return we told of a nice little spot just out from Coonabarabran, after our experience with the broken sleep in stopping in a rest stop beside the Newell Highway. Having dealt with the noise road trains we went out of our way to find a localized quiet stop over for future reference, calling into the local Information Centre which is always rewarding.

When we arrived into the free camp we had heard of, high in the mountains of the Eyre Peninsula, we did find it really excellent. Graced with solitude, gas BBQ's, beautiful scenery, solar lighting and with plenty of tables and chairs, a lovely shelter hut and lots of trees it was exceptional. Even with the pleasure of clean loo's it was just a brilliant spot. Who would in their right mind trade this for a caravan park and we are the only ones here.

FREE CAMP ON THE EYRE PENINSULA

It was around here that we clocked up our 2,000klm mileage and then we moved on into Port Augusta which we simply passed through and took a left down onto the Eyre Peninsula.

Port Augusta has a number of interesting places to visit the least of which is Homestead Park Pioneer Village, but we will save these for you to discover. We pushed on seeking the quiet solitude of the bush. However the colours of sunset are stunning and along with dawn, these times have to be my favourite part of the day.

THE SKIES OF THE SAVANNAH PLAINS

The land east of Port Augusta is a region of salt lakes where there are no permanent rivers. The soil is very porous and any water simply seeps into the ground to the subterranean aquifers. So while you will see broad flat soaks and what look like dry river beds, they are merely run offs causing erosion which move as quickly as they settle into the landscape.

The Eye Peninsula really quite intrigues me and we plan to spend two days exploring, particularly around the southern peak and western coast of the Peninsula as we move towards the west and our destination. This is not enough time to do the region justice but it does leave you with a taste to return.

Port Lincoln is at the end of the Peninsula and a wonderful place for a good feed of fish'n'chips. It truly is a mecca for the fish lovers. The Peninsula has 2,000klm of beaches along its shoreline and is home to Parnkalla, Nauo, Kookatha and Wirangu clans who live mostly around the towns of Port Lincoln, Ceduna and Yalata.

Southern right whales, many weighing in at 80 ton and their smaller males and calves can be seen in the breeding season, June to November, this in the bays at the head of the Nullabor and the Great Australian Bight. The whales come into the nursery as they play and feed along the cliffs. They can be viewed from the 100klm stretch that is the Bunda Cliffs and at Twin Rocks, both locally known.

The whale population has in some part recovered since whaling was outlawed and the southern right whale was listed as endangered as a species. The Northern Atlantic right whale was all but extinct as early as

WESTERN COASTLINE OF THE EYRE PENINSULA – LOCKS WELL BEACH

1750 and remains truly endangered to this day with numbers remaining in the low hundreds. Man will hunt these magnificent animals to extinction if given the opportunity. If it isn't our modern world, shipping lanes and ill considered fishing and hunting methods which kill them, it will be the harpoon of the meanest whaler.

As the whalers moved into the Great Southern Ocean in search of this beautiful creature, they began to threaten both species of the right whale. The whale population in the southern oceans was decimated in the years between 1830-1850. Then with the arrival of industrial whaling ventures in the 1900's this bought the species to the brink of extinction. In 1937 hunting was banned and the populations have struggled back in numbers. Some countries however do not comply with these bans and continue to slaughter these beautiful and yet still endangered animal, regardless of the consequence to their continued survival.

The Southern right whales do not venture into the northern hemisphere waters as they are unable to survive in the warm waters across the equator so they are unique to the southern oceans. It has only been since the 1960's that we have seen these magnificent creatures return to the shores of the southern ocean land masses. It is hoped that their numbers will continue to increase despite the hunters.

The temperature has now dropped dramatically and hovers now in the low 20C during the day and at night cutting down to 10C as we move into the weather systems crossing in from the Great Southern Ocean.

Exploring the Eyre Peninsula is a special delight and the wilder west coast is an exceptional place. The tail of the weather low moving across into Victoria has bought light rain and strong winds to the peninsula which they expect will ease by tomorrow. For the moment we are occasionally buffeted by gusts but then it doesn't help that we are perched on a cliff edge facing the roaring 40's at a place called Locks Well.

Locks Well Beach is one of those wild westerly beaches perched at the bottom of a breathtaking sandstone cliff, which also happens to be an infamous fishing beach. Its 283 steps to the beach, but Hubby recons it is 289 and I aren't about to climb them again to check.

The two largest tribal groups which lived on the Eyre Peninsula, The Nauo and Parnkalla peoples, and they originally figured the Europeans were visitors, though by 1840 it must have dawned on them that the visitors were actually colonizing the place and the trouble with the tribes and settlers truly begun. It was by the late 1830's that Europeans began to outnumber the Aboriginal people.

The Nauo and Parnkalla were a peaceful people in general who moved towards the coastal beaches in the summer and into the hills and mountains of the peninsula in winter. Clashes over the use and possession of tribal lands were as inevitable as they had been since the beginning of time and the migrations of man, be it tribal or settler.

The concept of theft; be it of land or goods is a provoking argument and native and colonist will protest their point. It is however a mute point and the might of the prevailing social structure will always win the day, and so it was.

The fight for existence and dominance between cultures was often brutal and unjust, but it is the loss of cultural diversity which is the most damaging of things. By the 1850's the Aboriginal population was decimated not only by warfare, but also by disease against which they had no immunity. The population of the clans dropped down to an estimate of some 10% of what the original population was. This was the result and the impact of European settlement, both penal (involuntary) and emigrant (voluntary).

THE GREAT AUSTRALIAN BIGHT

THE GREAT AUSTRALIAN BIGHT

The Great Australian Bight is said to be the longest line of sea cliffs in the world. Its starting point and finishing point are a bone of contention according to who you listen to but essentially for Aussies it starts s a few kilometres back at the point of the Eyre Peninsula in the east and stretches to Cape Pasley in the far west, a distance of some 1,170klm or 720 miles and it is now a large marine park or reserve which lies south of the Nullabor Plain. The Nullabor Plain covers some 77,000 sq. kilometres and is simply vast.

As we head into the Bight the cliffs facing the vast Southern Ocean are stunning and run easily along the shore except at this end where they are broken occasionally by lovely windswept beaches and a few fishing towns scattered along the west coast of the Eyre Peninsula.

The Eastern shores of the peninsula are much kinder than the western shores and the farming land is gentler with rolling farm land of yellowed grass which feed sheep and cultures wheat. You can catch glimpses of the azure waters of the Spencers Gulf as you travel along and there are a smattering of fishing village's right up to when you reach Port Lincoln, also known as the seafood capital of Australia.

Port Lincoln, as we found, is almost on the tip of the Eyre Peninsula but lends itself to the sheltered eastern shore. We spent a number of hours exploring the port and enjoyed ourselves immensely. However my aim was to gather some local foods to explore and we discovered a lovely store where I managed to get some beetroot skordahlia which made a lovely sauce for some linguine and this we enjoyed with a wasabi and herb marinated squid... it was gorgeous and it looked spectacular! Tomorrow I am hoping to get into the abalone which is local also.

Once we rounded the point of the peninsula it was like a different world. The farmland turned incredibly stony, so much so that the settlers began to build the paddock fences with stone reminiscent of Ireland and Scotland.

We came across many of the salt lakes of the region sitting like brilliant white patches on the landscape. Those cliffs also became more evident all

along the coast and the winds buffeted the little 'bitch box' along. The older houses here are mostly made of a sandstone blocks and they look charming and so much part of the regions character. You also occasionally get one of the blue stone houses, but not so often that they are not striking.

The soil is incredibly stony with so much sand stone that it is rare that you see enough land that is being cropped and the farms are mostly stocking sheep where the land isn't under salt lakes. It is a lovely region and I can't wait to move further up the western coast of the peninsula as there is much to see ahead of us yet.

The land about here brings to mind Jonathan Swift writings (1667-1745) and Gulliver's Travels. On a journey, aboard the 'Adventure' in 1703 he recounts the tale of the land of Brobdingnag. A land of giants to where he was delivered by a Southern Monsoon storm while in the frozen sea, to a great island or continent where the land he took to explore initially was all *'barrenland rocky'*, which to my mind aptly describes the land here about.

The sentiments Jonathan expresses when he is discovered by the giants of the land brings to mind the thoughtless way in which we treat and regard small animals and the like. By comparison, a harrowing tale particularly in his escape from this land at the mercy of an eagle in flight as it attempted to carry him to breakfast, one in which he featured as a mains course. I don't know how much of such a tale the pups understand but I hope it is a warning, aware as I am of the eagles that watch out for a satisfying snack.

Once again, Jonathon was South of *'New Holland'* (Australia, so named by the early by the Dutch seafarers) when he was rescued and you can appreciate the emotions the Bight engenders when you look out over the great expanse of the ocean and see the heavy, wild swells which crash up against the cliffs.

Tomorrow we hope to make Ceduna which isn't that far on, but there is way too much to see and we have to be selective if we are to get into Kalgoorlie when we plan. As we head up the west coast of the peninsula, we will be moving more towards the Nullabor landscape and this I am very much looking forward to.

We have really loved our tour along the Eyre Peninsula and are already talking of returning to the area. Tere is just so much to explore. But for the moment we are nestled safely in our little van listing to the song of the oceans roaring 40's and tonight we will be rocked to sleep for sure.

The new day bought us a glorious sky. The low has blown itself out and the skies are blue. It was so peaceful when we got up with the sunrise that we couldn't resist another assault on the stair case that leads down via the cliff face and onto the beach for a frolic along the sand.

THE PUPS ENJOYING THE SOFT SAND

The cliffs are all soft sandstone, as is the rocky ground; it is all based on sandstone and some of it quite fragile while other parts are very solid.

There is also a basalt conglomerate formations here and we visited 'Murphy's Haystacks' these are ancient wind-worked granite inselbergs which are over 1500 million years old and they sit in the middle of a paddock in isolated glory. There are a few of these inselbergs about and wandering amongst them is like shades of *'Picnic at Hanging Rock'* they are fascinating to photograph and such a contrast to the surrounding country which is best described as mulga and farmland.

But by far the most enjoyable part of the day was luncheon at the cliff edge above the sea lion colony.

This colony is at a little place called Point Labatt which has the only breeding colony of sea lions on the Australian mainland and the colony was quite healthy, with bulls, calves and mums and they were lovely to watch.

THE INSELBERGS AT MURPHY'S HAYSTACKS

The approach route was some 50klm of dirt track this each way. You travel out onto a peninsula and the little bitch box is now sorely in need of a clean and a screw up! But it was wonderful to be able to view the colony and we enjoyed lunch while watching the calves feed. I just couldn't resist taking pictures

We've also been exploring the subtle differences in the way South Australians say things. They called devon, fritz? Shades of a German heritage there methinks. They also have the strangest term for a *'bucket of ice-cream'* and the like; they call this a damby of ice cream... I might have spelt that wrong too but I was too chicken to venture the question which I doubt even had an answer anyway. Then of course there is the 'pie floater' which I believe is pie and peas.

There is also the Australian gnome; these are all Australian made and it is a response to the influx of garden gnomes made and imported from overseas... you know the ones I mean, those pretty little coloured guys. The Aussie ones are all Australian toned colours and are made by Aussie farmers in SA. They are new to the market and they are releasing them on

Sunday with a big shebang and are encouraging people to buy Australian made gnomes so they should be in the garden centres Sunday. They say they feed them (or they have in them) kangaroo droppings too as it is part of their make-up and if you water they are said to actually grow fatter.

I have taken the opportunity to buy some local abalone. It is collected around here and there are also a good deal of oyster framing which goes on amongst the fishing villages which are scattered all along the coast. The abalone when bought fresh is $145 a kilo... and no that isn't a typo. However as we plan on taking it into Kalgoorlie we got a preserved variety that is preserved locally and shipped to the Asian market. I haven't decided how I am going to serve it, although I have a good idea and I am very much looking forward to experimenting with this in cooking.

We are settled in at a caravan park at Ceduna and catching up with the washing and recharging batteries and giving the portable freezer a boost in prep for crossing the Nullabor. Tomorrow we should make it as far as Eucla near the border between South Australia and Western Australia. It is a trying run which will be relieved by photo opportunities along the head of the Bight, though it is too early for the migrating whales for which the area is renowned.

There is some debate about where the Nullabor road actually starts but the consensus is that it starts at the Nullabor Roadhouse which sits just inside the Nullabor National park. The roadhouse also is about 94klm from Yalata and adjacent to the historic Homestead. The actual road stretches some 720klm from east to west and while it is commonly thought that Nullabor is an aboriginal word, it isn't.

It comes from the Latin nullus and arbor meaning 'no trees' which is something of a misconception. It seems there is also some contention about the correct spelling, whether it could be Nullarbor, Nullabour, Nullabor or Nullarbour.

General consensus with the locals that we spoke to is that it should be Nullabor and they should know. For although its breakdown lends itself to 'arbor' in the Latin; 'arbour' as spelt by some in the English version of Latin and the addition of the 'null' part means 'no trees'. There are in fact bushes and trees on the Nullabor so in typical Aussie brashness we tend to negate the Latin meaning as it is incorrect anyway... so we invent our own.

I would have enjoyed visiting the caves along the way, however most of them you need a 4 wheel drive to get to so we have to pass on that and plan for another time. Few people realize the expanse of subterranean caves which exist under the plain. Surface evidence is usually simply a hole but these holes lead down to a whole other world.

For generations, cavers have enjoyed the experiences to be had in the subterranean lakes, rivers and caverns. Since so many lives have been lost though it is now necessary to obtain a permit to enter these places.

THE THYLACOLEO OR ANCIENT MARSUPIAL LION OF AUSTRALIA

Most recently in 2002 three simple holes in the ground of the plain led to a magnificent find. A cavern was discovered which harboured a graveyard of animals, many from the mega-fauna age when the plain was a vast forest of woodlands and savannah. Not unlike the mega-fauna of the Naracoorte caves in South Australia, the graveyard has produced an insight into an ancient land where the thylacoleo, or marsupial lion ranged along with the giant tree kangaroo and other animals of an ancient world. The site remains closed to date but in time it will be recognized for the treasure it is.

HTTP://WHEREIS.COM THE NULLABOR, CEDUNA TO KALGOORLIE

CROSSING THE NULLABOR

The Aboriginal name for the Nullabor is Oondiri... meaning place without water; I think that is very apt as while there are some scrubby tortured trees, there is definitely no water out here. None that isn't at the bottom of a cliff that is, or hidden deep beneath the ground in subterranean aquifer's and rivers flowing within the limestone.

The Nullabor, or Oondiri (which is more accurate a description) was lifted out from the sea to form a limestone plain of spectacular nothingness. The cliff edge of the plain is breathtaking (there are bloody big cracks back from the cliffs in the limestone too!!) There are simply no flowing rivers here at all which grace the surface but it is a different story beneath the ground.

Any water just seeps through the porous limestone to the subterranean caves and this is where the explorers of the day are at the moment finding a mine full of fossils

When you first embark back on the road headed west from Ceduna, what you notice most are the lovely old stone buildings crumbing away in disuse. While the land is an amazing view of rolling farm land that gives way after a time, to land that is quite scrubby. You have to pass through the Yalata Aboriginal Reserve which has been preserved as virgin scrub for

hundreds and hundreds of miles, where camels, dingoes and wild cats roam.

We can vouch for the wild cats... we saw more of these than dingo's which crossed our path as you all know what a cat looks like. This dingo pictured was skulking around looking for anything to eat. We have also been warned not to let the pups out tonight as the dingo's have a habit of stealing away domestic dogs and enslaving them to the alpha breeding pair, particularly in cross bred mongrels of dingo lineage. They help raise the litters and act as babysitters for the breeding pair, or the alpha pair of the pack.

In 1996 the Yalata Aboriginal Reserve through which the road stretches initially, was proclaimed an indigenous protected area. The reserve has the largest expanse of untouched coastal malley country in the southern hemisphere and is the lands of the Anangu people. Anangu is the term Yankunytjatjara and Pitjantjatjara Aboriginal people of these language groups from the Western Desert, as they refer to themselves.

The families descend from the desert people in the north and north-west regions in the spinifex country and they are committed to conserving the land. Early Anangu tribal settlers mined a band of minerals found between the limestone formations to extract and trade a hard and brittle chert that was used to make cutting tools. The

THE WILD DINGO

vast reserve covers some 458,000 hectares or 100,000 sq klm and is home to a community of approximately 400 people.

The question of Aboriginal Reserves is a poignant one, however I take the view that I would rather see the traditional owners of the land control their land than have multi-national interests move in and develop or destroy the land we love and value so much. Whether the development is for tourism or mining interests, the future of the land needs to be considered and not merely the economic advancement of investors interests which is often the case.

We have to be find a balance between traditional owners, Australians native and indigenous to the land and the often greedy push for development and industries often coined as 'progress' designed to cater to mining or tourism in many instances.

A balance also does not mean that anyone has a right of access or to use the land as they choose. A balance should be found between the land, its future and its current use. We should strive towards a balance, not a possession or monopoly by either interest. Those who should not have a say are those who merely visit our land with a view to taking without regard to the future of our land and the place our children will inherit. Too often the only say which is heard is that in encouraging development of resources and it seems this is where *pollies* have fingers in the pie mostly, or so it seems sometimes.

You require a permit to enter the Aboriginal Lands, should you choose to, and this is available from the Head of Bight Interpretive centre during the whale season. This runs according to commercial interests, from June to October each year. The Southern Right Whale visits this coastline on their annual breeding migration and they can be seen along the vast length of the Bight.

Once you are through the Aboriginal Reserve which is about 18klm east of the roadhouse and station house called 'the Nullabor Roadhouse', this is where the scrub begins to give way to the treeless plain and it is amazingly flat and seeming all nothingness. We are currently camped away from the cliff face around half way across the Nullabor and the cliff just plunges into the southern ocean not far from the highway here.

We spent the night tucked up in the little van listening to the buffet of the winds whipping up from the ocean, and across the Plain. One of few distractions along the way is the road signs and I couldn't resist stopping at the camel, wombat and kangaroo sign.

They should add a feral cat to that also but I doubt that sign exists. What is funny though is our pup 'Scruff Muffin' otherwise known as Scruff has just learnt to pee on trees, lifting his leg. He has a LONG way to go before the next tree!

The landscape of the Bight itself is fascinating and you can see why it is so famous, it just goes on forever. We have a few more spots to visit along the way yet of course but it would be hard to beat this view... the day was just perfect, not too hot and the sky was the most glorious blue for us.

We actually stopped and helped this bloke below to cross the road. He is a skink, one of the desert dwellers who live comfortably in this harsh environment.

Tomorrow we will cross over into Western Australia and pass through our second time zone on our journey we will be 2 hours behind the East Coast now but that's alright because the sun also sets 2 hours later. We also clocked up our 3,000klm today and I am hoping that Eucla in WA will have a phone uplink for communication, namely emails. There has been no network capability since we left the Eyre Peninsula believe it or not. Though we were warned of this I must admit.

We had hoped to visit some of the many subterranean caves you can find along the way. One in particular being Cockabiddy Cave which is where the desert floor has collapsed into a "void" revealing the subterranean aquifer that is underneath the Nullabor Plain, which is also one of the biggest subterranean lakes found to date.

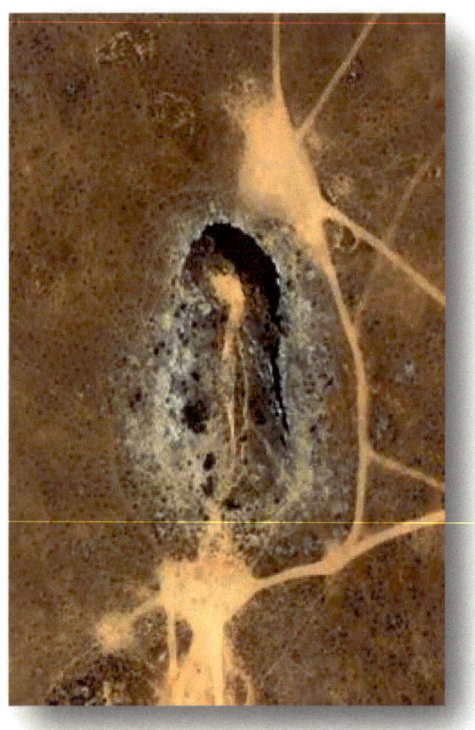

AN AERIAL VIEW OF COCKABIDDY CAVE

The Cockabiddy cave which is nearby has been closed to the public since a fatal accident a while back in which two cave divers lost their lives. National parks and wildlife are going to develop the area of the cave to make it safer we are told and as it is the only cave usually open to the public that is easily accessible I hope it is soon. Other cave sites require a four wheel drive to access them. I am disappointed that we couldn't visit the cave but this is something we can now save for another time.

Yesterday we visited a few rock sites, one namely Newmans Rock. These are simply immense rocks buried into the plain. It is the most unimpressive sight but very significant as these are the only sites across the Nullabor where water is naturally available. This, where ground water

OUR CAMP AT EUCLA

from the cold nights or infrequent rains, have not drained into the aquifers but stayed atop the rocks, storing this valuable resource. In days gone by this is how travellers found life sustaining water, in particular the afghan trains (camel trains) which were in the past the life line of the plains and Aboriginal tribal groups crossing the Oondiri.

Our journey across the Nullabor on the endless tar strip has bought a few surprises... firstly it is the camaraderie, something I never gave a thought to. We are on this journey of some three days with any number of people doing the same journey all going in the same direction. You run across these same people consistently and even get to know them at the 'photo opportunities' at the escarpment edge, and at the few petrol stops which you are forced to patronize if you want to make the trip. You also see them as well at the overnight stops, whether you chose the freebie stops or the few caravan parks at the road houses along the way. We found a camp at a freebie site currently, which is about 300-400klm west of Norseman, a spot which has shelter, loo's and water... the big three and out here that is very important.

We have collected a small circle of friends along the way these last few days and there are a few of us that seeing one or the other settled for the night, or even dropping into the 'photo opportunity' spots or perhaps snacking along the parking bays. New found friends will stop also, or toot, or wave madly and we tend to congregate and natter and it is like belonging to the family when you finally get to your third day... it is all quite comforting.

Scruff, our pup, is by far the most popular amongst these friends and has made a wide circle of acquaintances, amongst them a little girl who looks out for our van and insists the parents stop if they see us, so she can greet Scruff and have a play. Even Scruff now gets all excited when he sees her! I guess at Norseman we shall all go our separate ways and if we were one of the 'grey nomad' set we would continue on with the friends we have made. You would greet them as they make their way up north towards Broome and further on around the top end or south to Esperance thousands of miles away along the western coastline of Western Australia. However it is not our time yet... and we are viewed as the youngens gearing up to the national migration, which is somewhat all rather comforting.

Another surprising thing we have discovered is that while the Nullabor Plain itself extends to Norseman; you actually drop down off the plain at Eucla. Here you drop down through a pass onto a lower plain once you leave Eucla and you travel across this for a part of your journey. There is a stretch called the Hampton Tablelands, which are marginally higher than a coastal stretch known as the Roe Plain. Having crossed the Roe Plain you then go up through the Madura Pass back onto the Nullabor.

I have included a view of the tablelands and the Roe Plain, taken at the Madura Pass, it is quite striking methinks though the picture doesn't do it justice unfortunately. What was most intriguing also was to find sea shells up on the Nullabor escarpment... reason tells me that these sea shells must be some 25 million years old. They sit high on the escarpment and there is simply no access to the ocean... 25 million years!

THE ROE PLAIN

That is how long it has been since the Nullabor Plain rose from the sea and there is no way that anyone could have put that shell or any of the other thousands of shells there earlier, as there was no way down the cliff face…. 25 million years... the mind boggles.

We camped on the edge of the longest straight stretch of road in the world... being the stretch from Caiguna to Balladonia, 145klm of dead straight road, relieved only by a few obscure bumps in the road. Contemplating this as you viewed the scenery it seemed at times a tad monotonous though I will add that the sunsets are simply stunning.

Tomorrow we will pass through the Fraser Range and on into Kalgoorlie, it has been a great trip across the Nullabor and I hope you enjoyed it also. Research is an important part of travel and one of the greatest pleasures I had in doing the research for this trip was reading the account of Daisy Bates, who at the turn of the 1900's went out on the edge of the Oondiri Plain to live her life amongst the Aboriginal people who facing the colonization of their land found themselves dispossessed.

Daisy Bates is a woman you have to admire and if it wasn't for her work, her labour and her hardships we would know so little about the people of the desert and the Oondiri Plain.

She fed them, clothed them and nursed them through sickness. Daisy Bates was a true pioneering woman who is much to be admired. Her book, 'The Passing of the Aborigines' is an exceptional story of hardship and courage in the same vein as Bill Harney who also spent his life amongst the *first peoples* to this land.

The Aboriginal Serpent Lore of the Oondiri plain is also something I would chose to recognize. The *Kajoora Serpent*, is a dragon of the plain and little is known of this ancient Lore, except that the it is the call of the Serpent that you hear on the still nights, your ear to the earth as the serpent moves through the ancient caverns of the Dreamtime.

Known also by other names such as *Ganba* or *Jeedarra* he passes now into legend but you can still hear his movement in the caverns beneath the ancient land.

The Aboriginal people feared this serpent and would not cross the plains for this reason, staying instead mostly to the coastal fringes and the higher desert lands.

This is the land I love and I would choose to be nowhere else.

KALGOORLIE THE CITY OF GOLD

First a word about communications! There ain't any! We have travelled near the 1,000klm across the Nullabor from the Eyre Peninsula and not once did we achieve a telephone network link in the distance from Ceduna to Norseman, some 1,200klm and if anyone ever mentions 98% connectivity or phone coverage across Australia to me again they will get an ear full!

Finally we made it to the "City of Gold" (Kalgoorlie) and taking the time to wind back for the last day or two just taking it easy is a delight. Our trip into Kalgoorlie was interesting... coming in off the Nullabor Plains, it was striking to suddenly be climbing into the Fraser Mountains. Travelling from the flat salt bush and spinifex plain to ancient gum forests and undulating and hilly land offered a lovely diversion. We came in via Norseman which is a typical country town, small and personal which had quite interesting beginnings.

But that is another tale and as we head into the frontier town of the Western Desert I hope you have enjoyed the travelling. I surely have! And I would like to thank you for travelling with me.

I wanted to leave you with an image of Kalgoorlie, The Desert City of gold and as I searched my catalogues' of photo's, the pubs, the bordello's and representations of its history, the awe inspiring Super Pit of Gold... the choices were many.

In the end I chose a message of history. Above is a picture of a 'two-up' ring which can be found just out of Kalgoorlie in the red desert sands. Kalgoorlie is to this day a wild rich frontier town in a class of its own and this two-up ring is still used. Two-up is an illegal game in Australia, a simple toss of coins off a board and bets are placed on 'heads or tails' and the fall of the coin. But it is a game loved by our Anzac's and others, its simplicity is engrossing and the culture that surrounds it is equally addictive.

THE TWO-UP SHED

Under the law we are given licence to play the game only on Anzac day... this rink gets used more often than that but then it's hard for the Law to sneak up on a place in the desert that is as flat as a tack.

Join me in my tale of the 'Desert City of Gold' that is Kalgoorlie. And our trek back along the Nullabor in 'Out on the Never, Never, Never'. You will be simply surprised at the diversity of the tale.

We have since crossed the Nullabor many times, and have many tales to tell of our different journeys to other places. I hope you will enjoy the tale as much as I enjoyed the telling. Drop me a line via my website, I would love to hear from you.

'Till next time.

Jan

Visit Jan at http://janhawkins.com.au/Publications.html **and discover more about her travels and tales of Australia.**

By the same Author

The Dreaming Series

A story of fiction, adventure and love; a Series of four books which introduce the blending and balance that is so much part of the Australian Cultural experience. Meet the Spirit Creatures of Australia and the men and women who are so much part of the Dreaming and Dreamtime. Learn about the spirituality which is inherent in this Land Australia. Travel with the Aboriginal Shaman in their daily lives as they struggle to blend a ancient Lore with a modern land and the countries deep spiritual links with what is timeless... a time without time... a state that is the land itself, our Mother.

Visit Jan at http://janhawkins.com.au

www.ingramcontent.com/pod-product-compliance
Lightning Source LLC
Chambersburg PA
CBHW042007100426
42738CB00037B/22